Produced by:

Hubler Enterprise/UNDUN RECORDS
P.O. Box 41
Battletown, Kentucky U.S.A. 40104

The purpose of this book is to put forth ideas and suggestions of ways to possibly make America's vast system of roads and bridges last a little longer, or have an extension of useful life. Any reference to people, living or dead, or to any groups or organizations is not intended to be derogatory or demeaning. The ideas and suggestions in this book are expressed solely for constructive purposes to help our country, The United States of America.

Photo credit, front cover:
        Courtesy of Mike Wills - Flickr

Photo credit, back cover:
        Courtesy of Robert A. Eplett –FEMA

In Appreciation, My Special Thanks To:

JANET HUBLER, my sister – her help on this book is much appreciated

FRANK KING, ----- A very helpful friend

WIKEPEDIA, The online encyclopedia, --- a very helpful source of information

The MEADE COUNTY LIBRARY, Brandenburg, Kentucky, ---for their very nice place to work and research information

III

"A Reprieve Plan for Our Ailing/Failing Roads and Bridges"

By: Jim Hubler

I have been thinking of writing this book for quite a long time. Well now, its time has come. In the past few months' news has been released stating that America's Federal Highway Administration will run out of money sometime in late 20014. I'm sure that our government will find more money somewhere, somehow, but in the meantime we need to spend huge amounts of money to maintain and rebuild or replace many of our ailing roads and bridges. Until the financing for these projects is arranged, wouldn't it be commonsense to do some things that very well might result in some of our roads and bridges being usable and lasting a little longer? Thus, the reason I have written this book.

Contents:

Chapter 1

"The Condition of Our Ageing Roads and Bridges"

America, if you have it,
It probably came by truck,
That truck crossed many bridges,
Still standing just by luck.
If our bridges ever fail,
The trucks will come no more,
Then there'll be nothing left to buy,
In most any store!

To most anyone traveling on our Interstate Highways, it should be obvious that they, for the most part, are not in the best of repair. There are sections in various states that the pavement looks a lot like plowed ground. There are many reasons for this, even though most states are doing their best to keep the roads and bridges in good condition. However in many places the roads and bridges are deteriorating faster than they can be re-built. Of course, there are the lagging economy, and lower tax revenues coming in, which do contribute to the existing conditions out there. As well, everyone has heard of the horrors of the bridge collapse at Minneapolis, Minnesota, some time ago. That event alone makes many thinking people wonder about every bridge they cross, will it hold them up?

For the reader to have a better understanding of the number of bridge collapses in America, and worldwide, recently and in the past, please consider doing the following. Turn on your computer, and search online for the following on-line sites:

Bridge collapses images of bridge collapses List of bridge failures-Wikipedia- the Free Encyclopedia - This site is lengthy but very interesting and educational.

After checking out and studying these sites it should be obvious to most anyone that bridge failures are not 'fantasy land', or isolated incidents, and that they are real and do occur all too often. Now, you, the reader should have a much clearer understanding of what this book is all about. Please pardon me for 'side-tracking you', and please continue reading.

This book spells out a plan to at least help our ailing/failing roads and bridges to potentially last a little longer. No, it's not a plan for instant repair or re-construction, but rather a 'reprieve' of sorts, for they are currently under a 'death sentence', so to speak. There is no 'quick fix' now, and there will not be one later. This plan and these suggestions won't fix or repair anything, but would potentially buy a little added time, or an extension of useful life for our system of ageing ailing/failing roads and bridges. In short my suggestions could buy a little more much needed time for them. While it's true that my suggestions and plans are only temporary or 'stop-gap' measures it seems obvious that some changes need put in place, and soon!

This plan should cost our Country next to nothing, and could only help the current situation, how could that possibly be wrong? It could easily be managed by existing govt. workers and regulatory people. The main cost involved would be publicizing new rules, putting up new signs, which are usually made very economically in our prisons. As well money could be saved in the building of the signs by picking up soda and beer cans, thrown along our roadways by uncaring slovenly types, and re-cycling them into metal for the signs. Even further, perhaps these cans, etc., could be picked up by some of those paying their debt to society. The new signs would be regulating the new regulations. The plan shouldn't need to be ruled by a 'Czar', and yes in short, it's nothing more than a commonsense, conservative, belt and suspenders approach to a very serious problem. Ben Franklin is one of my 'heroes in history', and I love quoting him. Franklin said, "Common sense is all too un-common." I think we need to try to make common sense more common.

Should we fix that bridge now, or do it later?

"We talked about it long ago, but that's water under the bridge." "Oh, we'll cross that bridge when we come to it!"
"But what if the bridge is under the water?

Chapter 2

"History of Interstate Hwy. and Similar Roads"

But before going into this plan, let us go back to the history of The Interstate Highway System in America, as well as similar types of highway systems in other countries. The Interstate Highway System in the U.S.A. is not an original idea. Germany had conceived of a very similar system of roads back in 1913 to 1921, which was delayed by World War 1. It was known as the autobahn, and was finished in 1932. Most people credit Hitler for building it, but he didn't. However, it was very special to him because of its obvious military advantages. From its start in 1932 with 108 kilometers of road, to approx. 3,736 kilometers in length in 1940, the time during World War 11, that benefited Hitler the most. It was approx. 12,845 kilometers long or 7,982 mile long by the year of 2012. Italy had their version of an expressway type of road completed in 1923. It was 130 kilometers long and was named The Autostrada. In the U.S. Parkway System, the Pennsylvania Turnpike was opened in 1940 and was 162 miles long from Irwin, Pennsylvania to Carlisle, Pennsylvania. Now the Pennsylvania Turnpike reaches from Lawrence County Ohio to the New Jersey border, a total length of approximately 360 miles or 580 kilometers.

Our Interstate Highway system was started during the administration of President Dwight D. Eisenhower. It was named in his honor, The Dwight D. Eisenhower National System of Interstate and Defense Highways. Yes, the official name was lengthy. It was also known by other shorter names such as, Interstate Highway System, Interstate Freeway System, or simply, The Interstate. We were engaged in the 'cold war' at the time, and the possibility of nuclear war, or said another way; by being bombed by atomic bombs were a very real possibility. President Eisenhower could see the benefit of having the Interstate system to evacuate thickly populated areas more quickly in the event of atomic war. As well, the added benefit of being able to move food, troops and military equipment faster and easier if the need arose. Eisenhower being a dyed in the wool military man, insisted that the new highways have bridges strong enough for trucks carrying heavy army tanks, etc., to cross without any problems. Also, he insisted that all overhead clearances be at least 14 ft. high. This was determined to be just enough over the then legal maximum height limit which was 13 ½ feet in most places and allowing some inches for re-paving.

However in 1957, this height rule was changed to be 17 ft. because it was realized that our Atlas Inter Continental missals were too tall to be shipped on railroads and thus had to be moved on trucks. Later, this height rule was lowered to 16 ft. due to some transportation changes. This rule applied to all rural roads in the Interstate Highway System. The exception to this rule was that only at least one route in urban areas had to have overhead clearances of at least 16 ft. This would allow tanks and other military related equipment to pass under with no problems. The system was deemed to be in 'The National Interest'. There is no doubt that it was.

The, Federal Aid Highway Act of 1956 authorized the building of the Interstate Highway System. The sum of $26 billion dollars was authorized to build the initial 41,000-mile system of roads. As of year 2010, the system had grown to over 47,000 miles long. It took approx. 35 years to build the entire system. Of course that will grow as the population grows. The estimated cost of original construction was approx. $425 billion in 2006 dollars. It was funded 90% by the Federal Government, from truck fuel taxes etc., the rest to be paid for by truckers, and those who used it, as well as some paid for by states. As well, a so-called 'wheel tax' was imposed on trucks weighing 9000 # and over (empty weight) to help pay for construction and maintenance of the system.

The modern day version of this tax on trucks is called, Heavy Vehicle Use Tax. This tax applies to vehicles and combos, (semis etc) weighing 55000 pounds or more, when loaded, and traveling over 5,000 miles per year.

Chapter 3

"A Comparison of Heavy Trucks, Then and Now"

Now for the causes of some problems and their possible solutions: Back in 1956, when the Interstate system was started, the average gross weight of combination vehicles was around 56,000 pounds over most of the U.S. For the most part, roads and bridges were built to withstand these typical weights. Added to that the numbers of trucks using these roads was far fewer than now.

As well, truck speeds and speed limits were typically about 55 miles per hour. A few years later, the maximum legal gross weight of trucks and combos was raised to 72,000 pounds. Of course this depended on the number of axels and tire sizes and axel spacing on the truck rigs, but this was an increase in gross weight of approx. 28.57%. The bridges had been designed for fewer trucks and less weight. A few years later, the 72000 pound gross weight limit was raised to 73280 pounds. Still, many of the same bridges and road surfaces, but though a smaller increase of weight limits this time, (only an increase of approximately 1.77%), but an increase of approximately 30.85% increase from the original gross weight limit of 56,000 pounds, as before many of the same bridges, and many of the same road surfaces. After only a few more years, the

73,280 pounds limit was raised to 80,000 pounds; an increase from 73,280 to 80,000 pounds was 6,720 pounds, or an increase of approx. 9.50%. Yes, this was a larger raise this time, and to an increase of approx. 42.85% more than the original limit of 56,000 pounds. Yes, still using several of the same old bridges and road surfaces. As for the total weight increase from the original 56,000 pounds, we are now at 80,000 pounds, an increase of gross weight of, as said previously, approximately 42.85%. And yes, on many of the same old bridges and surfaces. To say that the bridges and lots of the roads are part of the original Interstate Highway System is not accurate. The original roads, for the most part, were designed to last around 20 years before completely re-paving. However, lots of parts of the system are 'original' or nearly so. There seems to be no easily obtainable data pertaining to the number of old bridges in the system. For that fact, their locations are not widely known. As well, it should be said that age does not necessarily destroy bridges, but excessive use and abuse certainly can do the job. As well, along with the typical 80,000 pound gross weight of truck and cargo, trucks are running faster than 55 miles per hour, usually much faster. These two things combined can result in roads and bridges getting a horrible beating.

While it's true that the heavier gross truck weights are being carried on more axels and tires, the fact remains that the gross weight being supported by the bridges is much more than what they were originally intended. Now, add to that the fact that there is now an estimated 20 times as many trucks using the roads as there was back in 1956 when the Interstate Highway System was started. Further, please remember, approximately 20 times more trucks, potentially with each truck weighing 42.85%, or 24000 pounds more than they did back in 1956.

Aside from the wear and tear and declining condition of our roads and bridges caused by all kinds of traffic, there are several more factors to consider. In the first place roads and bridges were never intended to last forever in the first place. Add to that the damaging effects of the weather and freeze and thaw. As well, extreme hot weather can cause some roadways to buckle and heave or in some cases sort of blow up. Yes, Mother Nature takes its toll as well. Also the damaging effects of salt and other ice melting chemicals to metal parts of bridges add to their shortened life. Consider all these factors and it's easy to start to understand why our system of roads and bridges are deteriorating faster than they can be rebuilt.

It's not that we don't have capable engineers and construction people, we are blessed with some of the world's best, it's a matter of not having enough available money to do these projects fast enough. Another contributing factor is that even though those in charge of our roads etc. see the need for much more maintenance and repair on our highway system. They are most often constrained by their superiors who in many cases prefer to spend money on 'pork barrel projects' in their home districts or in helping nations that will continue hating us, no matter how much money we give them. Said another way, most politicians are more interested in nation building in foreign countries, than they are in re-building our crumbling infrastructure here at home. Some of the re-building and repairs that needed done ten years ago didn't happen. Now ten years later, costs of everything involved is multiplied at least three times. Added to that will is the cost of repairing ten more years of damage caused by putting it off. If it needs fixed, it needs fixed now, putting it off is a 'no brainer', and it only ends up costing more. One case is in Louisville, Ky., on the Ohio, River Bridge. When they finally did get around to it, painting and repairs amounted to around one third of the original cost of the bridge. Of course, the needed time to do all the needed maintenance and construction is a factor as well.

It is undeniable that large trucks do the most damage to our roads and bridges. As shown before, it is laughable to think an automobile, weighing between three or four thousand pounds could cause as much wear and tear as a large semi with a gross weight of eighty thousand pounds. Of course, truckers and trucking companies are quick to say that they pay the Lion's share in taxes, road use fees, etc., which they do. But in any case, no matter who pays, the road and bridge system is not being rebuilt fast enough.

Chapter 4

"Considering the Weights on Our Bridges"

Now let's talk about some heavy weights on bridges, back then, and now. Back in the late fifties, when the Interstate Highway system was started, the typical maximum legal gross weight for heavy trucks was 56,000 pounds in most states. Now also remember there were a lot fewer heavy trucks on the roads back then. Now, the typical maximum legal gross weight for heavy trucks is 80,000 pounds in most states. As said, it has been estimated that there are now approximately twenty times more large trucks on our roads now, as opposed to back in the mid to late fifties. Those in charge of making weight limits and rules pertaining to bridges are not 'dummies' by any means. They have carefully formulated rules regarding truck/trailer combination lengths, weights allowed to be carried by axels, as well as length and space between axels. The rules are well thought out, for they 'spread' the weight out on bridges, keeping too much weight from being concentrated in one area, thus theoretically lessening strain on bridges. In addition to this, even if trucks are long enough, with proper spacing between their axels, which make them conforming to the 'bridge/spread rules', the situation could work out much better (pertaining to strain on bridges), if as well, the trucks would spread out, or stay farther apart. The 'bridge law' rules are well and good, but I think another step needs to be taken. The best 'bridge law' would be to make new rules about spreading out trucks on bridges, and then, strictly enforce those rules. Yes, there are already rules pertaining to how close trucks are allowed to follow one another, but largely it seems these rules are ignored all too often, especially on bridges. These rules need to carefully re-considered and implemented and enforced. When large heavy trucks are too close together, either moving or in traffic jams situations this can amount to massive weights on bridges in too close of an area. A commonsense idea would be to make a 'space rule' of perhaps 200 feet for moving trucks and 100 feet for trucks sitting still. Of course, such a rule regulating distance between trucks in various places probably wouldn't be a 'one size fits all' type of rule. Obviously different conditions might require even greater distances between trucks, for the sake of some bridges. This to be worked out by the traffic and highway engineers who are experts on this subject, this all being worked out considering bridge and bridge surface conditions. Our country is blessed with skilled people quite capable of making such decisions. I am only trying to make helpful suggestions and I am not qualified to do so. I am only relying on my years of trucking experience and my observations on roads, bridges etc., during those years. As well as, being at risk of becoming repetitious again; 'common sense'.

Next, for the sake of comparison, if ten large semis were on a bridge, end to end, the approximate total weight on the bridge would be around 800,000 pounds, or 400 tons. Of course if there were twenty large semis (on the bridge, side by side in two traffic lanes), the approximate total weight on the bridge would be around 1,600,000 pounds, or 800 tons. However, the number of heavy trucks on the road back then was far less than now, and the possibility of this much weight (20 large trucks), being on a long bridge at the same time would have been very unlikely. Considering the huge number of large trucks on the roads these days, the possibility of this happening could be very likely.

Another subject that I think needs touched on is that of trying to educate the average motorist about the massive weights involved with a large eighteen wheeler. For the purpose of comparison, let's say that the average automobile or pick-up truck weighs in the neighborhood of 4000 pounds, or 2 tons. Typically, the large semi-truck, when fully loaded often weighs as much as 80,000 pounds or 40 tons. It shouldn't take a Rocket Scientist to realize that truck very possibly weighs as much as 20 times the weight of your car or pick-up truck. Even so, some motorists seem to think they are on equal footing with the big trucks and take great risks doing so.

Now, back to the comparisons of weights on bridges. For example, if five average sized cars were bumper to bumper on a bridge, this would be approximately the length of one large tractor trailer, and the combined total weight of the five cars would be in the neighborhood of 20,000 pounds on the bridge in the same length of space. A large semi, fully loaded, would probably weigh up to 80,000 pounds or four times as much as the combined weight of five cars. Obviously small vehicles don't strain the bridges very much but large trucks can and do. So, again, big rigs should be required to maintain a certain distance, (set by law), on bridges whether moving or setting still. This distance should be worked out by our highway professionals or highway engineers. Of course this distance could vary according to bridge and road conditions. If these rules were passed and strictly enforced, there is little doubt that our bridges could, or should, last a little longer, in effect giving them a 'reprieve' or a little longer usable life. Of course this would not re-build the bridges or roads. That will take lots of time and huge amounts of money. The above suggestion is only a commonsense, short-term solution to a long-term problem. Once again, Ben

Franklin said, "Common sense is all too uncommon."

I know the following is 'ancient history', but even as late as the nineteen fifties, some bridges on two lane roads in Illinois and Iowa were known to be weak and were posted with low weight limits. As well, some had signs saying, "Only one truck on the bridge at the same time". This rule was enforced. I realize that our modern day world is moving much too fast for this sort of thing, but who knows? This kind of thinking could possibly come in handy in extreme circumstances.

Chapter 5

"Destructive Effects of Weight and speed etc."

Now, I've shown the possibilities of huge amounts of weight straining a bridge to the max! But remember, this theoretical example was of large trucks sitting still. Here is something else to think about, what if the road surface on the bridge had rough spots, potholes etc., and instead of sitting still, the trucks were moving at high speed? When heavy truck tires bounce over rough spots on road surfaces, this causes sort of a 'battering ram' or rebounding effect, resulting in more potential road surface damage, and on bridges, potentially damage to the entire structure. Of course higher truck speeds result in a much more severe pounding of the road surface. Yes, of course, potentially resulting in greater damage. I do not recommend that anyone should go under a bridge under a super-highway, but just being close and listening will illustrate the next item. When in hearing distance under one of these bridges, notice the resulting sounds when large trucks cross. Part of the loud noise is usually the expansion plate on the bridge, this is normal, however other loud bangs, cracks and so on are not normal and can be the sounds of damaging blows to the bridge. There are two simple remedies to cut down on lots of this bridge road surface and bridge damage.

Both are 'common sense' ideas, would cost nothing other than some signs, and could result in the bridges lasting a little longer or as I say, "Giving them a reprieve". The first suggestion is, 'Think Space', no; I don't mean the stars, Mars or outer space. I'm saying, "Space them out, make large trucks stay at least 200 ft., or more if necessary, apart on bridges, no matter if they were moving or sitting still!" This would result in the weight on the bridge being spread out more and not concentrated on such a close area. This would result in less strain on bridges and could or should give them a longer useful life, or a sort of reprieve. The second suggestion is, "Slow Them Down". When large heavy trucks go slower the result is less bouncing on even smaller imperfections in the bridge road surface. So, common sense, the rougher the road, the slower the better. These previous two suggestions together should help a growing problem. No, doing these things will not rebuild or repair bridges. But should result in a 'reprieve' for some currently under a 'death sentence'.

If implemented, these suggestions could hurt nothing. Remember, we already have the regulatory and Law Enforcement people to enforce these rule changes. Also, I'm sure we already have the people and facilities to make the needed signs. I'm referring to prisoners and prison workshops.

Chapter 6.

"Some Possible Remedies by Re-routing"

To say that our entire system of roads and bridges is failing or has failed is incorrect. However far too much of the system is headed in that direction. Here is another commonsense suggestion to possibly help give a 'reprieve' to some sections that are headed for trouble in the near future. Our country's many highway engineers are not dummies. Those that have been doing their jobs, as most have, are well aware of which bridges and roads are most likely to fail, or at least need massive repairs all too soon. Why not let them make recommendations as to what areas need relief from extremely heavy volumes of truck traffic? Then work together countrywide with other engineers and planners and trucking companies to figure out ways of re-routing part of this heavy volume of truck traffic to lessen the strain on our infrastructure. Again, common sense = Ben Franklin. Our bridges need to 'get a break, not get broken!' In many cases if different routes are used farther back in a long trip, the end total of miles often is not many more miles. Sometimes the total is even less miles by just using different roads. This is just one of many ways we could give an extension of useful life, or 'reprieve', to our ailing/failing roads and bridges.

Again it would or should cost very little, and would not require a departmental 'Czar', just some commonsense planning.

Perhaps as an added incentive for truckers and trucking companies to voluntarily start doing some re-routing to give some of our 'ailing/failing roads and bridges' a break lets consider the following suggestion. Why not give those that would participate, some sort of a small tax incentive for doing so. Even when re-routing added on a few more miles, then the tax incentive could compensate for going those extra miles. The expected/projected benefit of some roads and bridges having a little longer useful life would surely cover or offset the cost of a small tax incentive given to voluntary re-routers. Here once again, 'common sense', no big effort, just paperwork and agreements. I'm sure we already have the people in our governmental systems to handle the paperwork.

Chapter 7

"An Overview of Bridge and Road conditions"

One case in point, in 2010 Road Engineers in the state of Pennsylvania, reported that bridges on state, county and city roads had gotten in much worse condition since the last survey back on 2006. In only 4 years they were in much worse condition. By August 2013 they were in the process of restricting weight limits on approximately 1,000 bridges and, in some cases, reducing allowable weights on bridges by as much as 20 per cent. Yes, these were not bridges in the Interstate Highway System, but it is food for thought. Could our Interstate Highway bridges be suffering the same problems?

It was reported in 2013 that only approximately 38% of our nation's roads are in good condition. Also it is said that about 1 in 10 of our bridges, 20ft. or longer, are structurally deficient. As well around 14% of our nation's bridges are "functionally obsolete". The previous information was according to The U.S. Department of Transportation, and reported to Congress in 2010. It is also estimated that even though around $165 billion was spent on trying to upgrade our highway system in 2008, our nation would need to spend around $85 billion every year upgrade our roads and keep them in top shape.   Needless to say, that is money that we don't have, at present.

The government is now planning to add on some gasoline and fuel taxes to be earmarked for infrastructure repairs and upgrades in the system. Of course that is a start, but it will all take time. Obviously we still need to make our roads and bridges last a little longer. Despite all the money spent, our road condition, overall, was worse by 2011 than the bad conditions in 2008, by approximately 1%. Admittedly that's not much worse, but think, where did all those billions go, and what did we gain?

There are 5 states, Pennsylvania, Iowa, Oklahoma, Rhode Island, and South Dakota where at least 20% of their bridges are structurally deficient or need major maintenance or repairs. These bridges are in such a condition that they must be inspected annually to be allowed to stay in use.

Originally most Interstate Highways were surfaced to last around 20 years, after which re-paving and more repaving on top of the old was done. Now the authorities say in particular, that part of Interstate 70 close to St. Louis, Missouri, has been re-paved so many times, that the original road base is crumbling, and the road will need to be completely re-built soon. Of course, everyone knew from the start that roads and bridges weren't built to last forever in the first place.

Just to show differences in road and bridge conditions in different areas of our country, let us compare 3 states:

Alabama has approx. 9% poor or deficient bridges, around 8% poor roads, just over 25% fair roads, and a very good 66% of roads in good condition.

Iowa has approx. 21% poor or deficient bridges, around 23% of their roads are poor, around 41% of their roads are in fair condition, and only about 35% of their roads are considered in good condition.

California has approximately 12% poor or deficient bridges, just over 36% of their roads a rated as poor, around 42% of their roads are in fair condition, and a dismal 21% of their roads are considered to be in good condition.

In this comparison of these 3 states, Alabama stands tall!

I couldn't find the statistical ages of bridges in the Interstate Highway System, but I did find the following information and I found it to be very interesting. The average age of a bridge in America's system of roads and bridges is 42 years. Now, this isn't the average age of Interstate bridges, just bridges in America's road system as a whole. The following should make us all sit up and take notice! It is said that approximately 200 million trips are taken daily, (yes daily), across deficient or sub-standard bridges in our nation's

102 largest metropolitan areas. Could this possibly be the right time to get serious about saving our infrastructure? Or, should we just wait and cross that bridge when we come to it? Well, perhaps if it's still standing!

Perhaps this is a good time for the reader to play a little multiple-choice game:

Finish the following statement by choosing one to go with it that seems to be the most appropriate:

We will cross that bridge when we come to it,

1. If it's still standing.
2. If we have the nerve.
3. If it lasts that long.
4. Or maybe we won't.
5. But only after close inspection.
6. Perhaps, perhaps not.
7. If it seems safe enough.
8. Or we might find a way around it.
9. if that big truck ahead of us doesn't cause it to collapse

Chapter 8.

"Suggestions for Back-up Plans for Bridges"

For the sake of discussion, lets think, what if too many or several of our bridges were to start failing to the point that they were not usable. What if natural disasters or even terrorists were to destroy much needed bridges in our country and cause massive gridlock? I'm sure our leaders have a plan, of some sort, in case this was to happen. I have no way of knowing what their back-up plans are, but here are some of mine.

Have you ever heard of a "Bailey Bridge"? I'm sure most people haven't heard of them, they were used for military purposes, mainly in the era of WW 11. The inventor of the Bailey bridge was a British Army Corporal, Donald Bailey. He developed/invented a specially designed pre-fabricated bridge, composed of pre-fab panels of ingenious design. Though simplistic it was an Engineering marvel. It was designed to be assembled by using only manpower in some of its various assemblies. These bridges are held together with large pins installed with hand tools. Others could be assembled only using very little machinery. The Bailey Bridges are built so it's very easy to multiply component panels and assemble a bridge that will support heavy loads, heavy tanks, heavily loaded trucks, etc. Though they aren't really designed for high-speed traffic, in a pinch they work great. I have had some experience with these bridges during U.S. Army Combat Engineer's training. The Army still has hundreds of these bridges, I'm quite sure. As well, it's very likely that all branches of our armed forces have them or have access to them. Compared to the time it takes to construct a standard type of bridge, which can be weeks, months or longer, a Bailey Bridge can be assembled in just a few hours. In a time of disaster or too many bridges failing in a short time span, using Bailey Bridges would be the best quick term, temporary solution. Again, it needs to be said, it would be the most commonsense solution. I feel sure our leaders know this.

Also, concerning Bailey Bridges, America is lucky that some of our industries are still in our country. Bailey Bridges Inc., Fort Payne, Alabama is still in business and still manufacturing all components of these bridges. As well, they keep a large supply of bridge components in stock especially for the U.S. Army. Also they build replacement parts for the Army as needed. Bailey Bridges Inc. has a very good web site on the internet. It is very easy to understand, very informative, and very educational. Actually it would take a fair sized book to display all the information on their web page. It's well worth checking out.

Now, have you ever heard of a type of bridge known as a pontoon bridge? Pontoon bridges are merely decking, or planks or flooring of one kind or another, laid from one floating pontoon to another. Simply said, nothing more than a bridge surface supported by intermittent floats. The pontoon bridge concept is nothing new. One of the most famous pontoon bridges was ordered built by Xerxes1 of Persia in 480 B.C. in a war with Greece. The Romans made many versions and variations of pontoon boats or floats for use in pontoon type bridges, and used them quite successfully in a number of places. The Romans made one of logs to cross a large river in ancient times in a war with what is now Germany. During the American Civil War, they were used many times with good results. For the most part, these were nothing more than large row boats moored to a line across a river with bridge decking laid from boat to boat. Yes, they used them, and they worked. In later times they consisted of decking placed over barges or boats larger than rowboats.

The modern day pontoon boats used by our Army are basically huge rubber floats filled with air with prefabricated decking panels laid over them. A pontoon bridge built in this manner, can easily support heavy tanks, heavy trucks and many other types of traffic. Again, they are not for fast moving vehicles, but can and will do the job. The Army has a stockpile of these floating pontoon bridges, and could be used if needed in an emergency.

Another variation of the Army's floating pontoon bridge has, and can be used in the manner of a ferryboat. Though not fast, this will work. They simply connect the needed number of pontoons covered with deck panels, and add an outboard motor or motors if needed. The floating pontoon bridge is now a ferryboat of sorts. I've seen this done in training exercises, hauling tanks, loaded trucks etc. This will work.

I'm sure our leaders and emergency planners have already thought of this, but just in case they haven't, consider this idea. There should be a survey of the number and location of old or older ferryboats in our country. If any are scheduled to be scrapped, that should be changed, do not scrap any that could be made usable. The government should acquire a suitable number of these old ferry boats, put them in usable condition, keeping them in usable condition. Keep them in reserve for emergency use if needed. Yes, this would cost some money, but could be a bargain in the long run.

And yes, let's not forget about our Navy's LSTs and Troop Landing Craft which could be put in use if needed.

Another very important part of our system of roads and bridges absolutely should not be ignored. I am referring to the bridges still standing that has been bypassed by the newer generations of bridges. It seems to me that this is a 'no-brainer'. We need to maintain these bridges and keep them in usable condition. Some wouldn't necessarily need to be open to traffic, but be available in case of need. Yes, in an emergency, detours, etc. might be needed to take advantage of them, but in a crisis they could be a very valuable asset. Yes, this is a 'belt and suspenders approach but what's wrong with that? As wise old Ben said, "Common sense is all too common". These are just a few alternate or possible back- ups concerning bridges that could be used in times of need. Yes, they would all slow the traffic down but could and would work.

Chapter 9

"Some Lane Change Suggestions"

I know that my next suggestion will cause some flack, but it's so simple that it will work without a doubt. As well, if implemented, it would cost nothing or add to the National Debt. In addition it could help roads and bridges to potentially last longer. Yes, again, a 'reprieve' so that existing roads and bridges could have a little more useful life, and last a little longer. As before, highway engineers etc. from across the country need to survey the excess wear on roads due to requiring heavy trucks to use the right hand lane, or two right hand lanes or whatever. In areas where road surface damage is more than the automobile lanes, and in most cases it will be, make some very simple changes. Simply put up signs, yes, those cheap ones made in prisons, making heavy trucks use, or stay in the left lanes that formerly used to be for automobiles. Again, common sense = Ben Franklin. You do remember that he said, "Common sense is all too uncommon"? Yes, I know that change is usually not well received, but remember the potential savings for our country. Of course many will say this change would be dangerous, but please remember that those truckers are professionals, and quite capable of mastering this rule change. For one thing, they usually are not hindered by too much college education.

Most truckers are educated in the School of Hard Knocks and on the highways of life. Just surviving on a daily basis is a challenge. I'm quite sure that they could handle lane change rules.

Chapter 10

"Overloads Are Not the Main Problem"

The popular notion that overloaded trucks hauling massive overloads are the main culprits causing road damage just isn't so. This is true for several reasons. However this could change in the future. There are truck weigh stations strategically located on most all Interstate Highways, and most other major highways. In addition to that, most states put weight restrictions on a great many of the routes that could be used to bypass or avoid the truck scale locations. If a trucker gets caught 'dodging scales', especially on a road he is not supposed to be on, he is in trouble.

Another not too well known fact is that most large facilities that ship products by truck, especially bulk products, make trucks weigh in empty and weigh again when loaded. Very few will give a trucker a bill of lading showing gross vehicle weights that are illegal or over the limit. The main reason is that the modern laws make the shipper of the product liable right along with the trucker. So, the shipper requires the trucker to 'get legal', before he can leave the facility. It has been this way for several years. Most truck overloads are actually un-intended or accidental, these usually happen when a truck is loaded somewhere where there are only facilities to load product and no facilities or way to unload an accidental overload. Well, the freight rates on many lower paying bulk commodities are so low that deliberate overloading to make a few more dollars, just isn't worthwhile.

Another little-known fact, concerning trucks loading grain and farm products on the farm is that most states realize that what constitutes a load is partly guesswork. In view of that, many states allow gross weight and axel weight tolerances of sometimes between 3% and 5%.

Now, let me go back to what I said about truck weigh stations earlier, about possible changes in the future. I am told that some states are closing all or part of their truck weigh stations. They attribute lower revenue coming in through fines for violations, along with high operating costs in this lagging economy, as reasons for these closings. I have said, and still say that most truckers are decent honest people and won't take advantage of the temptation to violate the law. However the scale closings, in my opinion, amounts to an 'open-invitation' to those seeking to cash in by overloading the bridges.

Of course there will be those who will abuse the system and this could very well result in more road and bridge damage.

Regarding truck weight limits on our roads, I believe the weight limits are plenty high at the present time, in relation to the condition of our roads and bridges. I say that any movement to raise the present weight limits higher should be stopped in its tracks. The system is deteriorating fast enough the way things are now. In some cases I believe the weight limits on large trucks in certain areas should possibly be lowered.

Chapter 11

"The Reason for So Many Large Trucks Now"

One of the reasons that there are so many large trucks on the roads these days is this. Have you ever heard of a concept in the trucking industry referred to as 'J.I.T.'? JIT is an acronym that stands for 'Just in Time' delivery, (usually). Basically the concept is this: The factories don't want the materials or products in their warehouse or factory very long before using the materials or products. They want it basically delivered 'Just in Time' to be used as needed. This reduces warehouse costs by getting timely delivery to their production facilities, generally directly to their production lines. It saves dollars by avoiding extra handling. In some cases it could even avoid inventory being taxed when stored in a warehouse too long. So, now, we start to understand part of the reason for the vast numbers of large trucks on the road. Of course, this increased number of trucks on the roads does their part in wearing out the roads. In effect, that big rig there beside you, very likely is a 'rolling warehouse'. What used to be a warehouse is now rolling down the road beside you.

Since that rolling warehouse is trying to get to its destination, usually just in the nick of time, this often creates another problem. The truck driver is in a bind to be there on time, because his people promised it would be there on time. Often snow or ice or other road and weather conditions make arriving on time much more difficult. Now, we start to understand the obvious sense of urgency displayed by some of these up-tight Truckers.

To sum it up, the concept of scheduling materials to arrive more or less just in the nick of time at the production line, or the JIT concept, is probably here to stay. Yes, a large part of the large trucks on the road are now essentially 'warehouses on wheels' that used to be stationary warehouses. In view of this, common sense should tell us that these huge numbers of large trucks, or 'rolling warehouses', are here to stay and will probably continue to contribute to wear and tear on our infrastructure. As well, the more our nation's industrial base grows, more and more of these rolling warehouses will be on the road, it's only common sense. The ideas put forth in this book could help the situation some, but I think additional innovative ideas are needed.

Chapter 12

"Shipping by Rail Could Help"

Using alternate transportation modes is a four-star answer to giving our existing roads and bridges a reprieve, or an extension of useful life. If even a few more railroads were brought back, and if more freight was shipped on existing railroads, our existing roads and bridges could certainly last longer. As a thought comparison of truck transportation vs. railroad transportation, consider the following. In general, a modern rail car can carry approximately 112 tons, (224,000 pounds net weight), Using the maximum truck gross weight law of 80,000 pounds maximum gross weight, with each truck carrying an average 26 ton, (52,000 pound) load, in general it would take approximately 4 semis to carry the weight of the cargo in just 1 rail car, with 8 tons left over. Now, consider that modern rail trains are often 100 cars long. Now, for this comparison, it would take approximately 435 tractor-trailer rigs, grossing 80,000 pounds each, to haul what one 100 car train hauled. As well, some trains are often longer than 100 cars long. Think about it, a train operated by a crew of two men, compared to 435 truck drivers. And this is provided that the truck drivers were not long distance two man teams, think of the fuel used, and the potential pollution caused by 435 trucks, as compared to a couple of locomotives. Then, the clincher, think of all the potential wear and tear on roads and bridges caused by 435 heavy loaded rigs. You don't have to be a rocket scientist to understand that between the two, trucks and railroads, it's 'no contest'. Of course, somewhere in this equation trucks would probably be involved in some of the final delivery, but most of it would involve only short hauls. The downside of all this is the fact that too many railroads have left the scene and no longer exist. Too many people gave up on the railroads much too soon. Yes, obviously there needs to be a resurgence of railroad building.

I realize that I'll probably be compared to 'Benedict Arnold' for writing this, comparing trains and trucks, because I am a second generation truck driver and I was a trucker for approximately 43 years. As much as I hate to say it, facts are facts, roads and bridges are failing much too fast for the increasing numbers of trucks on our highways. Remember, its been estimated that there are now about 20 times the number of trucks on our Nation's roads, than there was when the Interstate Highway system was started in 1956. I don't have a crystal ball, but I'm betting that if we think there are too many trucks on the road now, we ain't seen anything yet! That should be obvious.

The railroad Piggyback system is good in lots of ways and should be used more. The railroad Piggyback system is the system that carries highway type semi trailers on flat bed rail cars. Usually two semi trailers are carried on one flat bed rail car. The system has strategically located staging areas where the semi trailers are either loaded onto, or taken off the flat cars. Yes, semi truck tractors are needed in this Piggyback mode of transportation, but usually only for shorter distances. Now, consider that a 100 car train, (some trains have more cars) carrying two semi trailers per flat car results in 200 semi tractor trailers not using roads and bridges on longer trips. Usually these a much shorter hauls. Again, this results in helping to give a reprieve to our ailing/failing roads and bridges of which too many are currently under a death sentence.

Have you ever heard of or seen a Road Railer Train? It is a concept that uses specially made highway type semi trailers constructed to sit on railroad bogeys, (sometimes called railroad trucks) which are basically tandem axels with railroad wheels. After these special made trailers are lifted and set on the railroad bogeys and attached and locked, the highway axels and wheels are raised upward by air pressure and locked in the up position. The trailers are then coupled end to end, and they form a Trailer Train. A typical Trailer Train has 125 trailer units in the train and can carry an approx. total weight of 4,800 tons of cargo. The train can be pulled by one locomotive. This concept has been tried and gone through many changes and improvements since first tried back in the 1950s. The trailers for Trailer Trains are made by the Wabash National Co. at Lafayette, Indiana. Triple Crown Services, and Triple Crown Trucking seems to be the biggest user of this unique concept. It seems to work very well. Although some trucks are necessary, they are usually only needed for shorter trips. This is, in my opinion the concept of the future. Think of it, 1 Trailer Train, 125 fewer trucks on the road, less pollution, and less wear and tear on our ailing/failing roads and bridges resulting in a potential longer useful life for our infrastructure. As I've already noted, we can't begin to replace or repair our roads and bridges as fast as they are going down. Who knows, perhaps commonsense is becoming a bit more common? Ben Franklin would surely be proud.

Another concept concerning railroad transportation needs to be revived, enlarged, and tried in other areas. Aside from people living in the Eastern U.S., very probably lots of people have never heard of Amtrak's Auto Train. In this mode of travel, your automobile is loaded aboard a special enclosed railroad car, they are called Auto Racks. However, it is not just limited to autos, RVs, motorcycles; small trailers can be taken as well. The automobile's owner and even his passengers ride in comfort in coaches, Superliner cars or roomettes. There is a dining car which serves food that is second to none. Also there is a lounge car. The Amtrak Auto Train runs from Lorton, Virginia, (near Washington, D.C.) to Sanford, Florida, (near Orlando). The 855mile trip takes around 19 hours, through Virginia, North Carolina, South Carolina, Georgia to the destination of Sanford, Florida. The automobile owner and his passengers arrive in comfort, well rested and well fed. No miles were put on the car; no money was spent on gasoline. As well, they had avoided dangerous driving conditions on overcrowded highways. Of course traveling on Amtrak Auto Train was safer also because there was no chance of colliding with someone talking on a cell phone, or texting at the same time they were pretending to drive.

And yes, there are a couple more pluses to traveling this way as opposed to air travel. First, you didn't have to pay extra for the extra luggage in your car, or carried onboard the train, as you would have on an airline. Second, when you get to your destination, you don't have to rent a car, you have your very own car there with you. Yes, it's still full of gas because it rode down with you. I think this mode of travel should be expanded to other areas and even promoted big time, perhaps even get some Govt. help. This type of system could conceivably be enlarged to run coast to coast or? I say, "Why not?" Instead of agonizing about space travel, wouldn't this be better for everything and everyone concerned? Again, all of the above would be giving some help to our ailing/failing roads and bridges, which need all the help they can get, even fewer automobiles on the road.

Here is another thought, regarding railroads. What if the government was to give a tax incentive to those that ship by rail? This could potentially increase rail traffic. This in turn could lessen the amount of trucks on our ailing/failing system of roads and bridges and in effect result in a 'reprieve' or longer useful life for our roads and bridges. Obviously we don't have the money or the time at present to fix all that needs fixed. If we did, it would all be fixed, or in the process of being fixed as we speak. Much to our country's shame, shortsighted people stood by and did nothing as a large part of our railroad system was either dismantled or abandoned. Wouldn't it be fair for our government to start helping re-build the railroads, and spend less time and money on re-building foreign countries that will continue to hate us, no matter how much money we give them? Really, which would be the most beneficial? Should we help our own country or help a foreign country that is all too often ungrateful for the help? As well, a resurgence of railroad building and construction could be a huge help to America's current high rate of unemployment. Once again, remember, Ben Franklin, "Common sense is all too uncommon".

Another thing that is often forgotten is the fact that charity should begin at home. Tend to our country's needs first, then worry about helping other countries. All too often we seem to have this reversed.

Chapter 13

"Shipping via Our Waterways"

America's river and lake transportation system is our nation's most under-rated, under-appreciated and overlooked mode of transportation. Actually, this ship by water system is a 'National Treasure', but this is understood by a precious few. Nothing we have, or are ever likely to have can even come close to competing with this water transportation system. They can move colossal amounts of weight at cheaper rates than any other system. While it's true river tow boats and barges are slow, as in lots of things a little thought and advance planning can result in huge savings. As well, giving some thought to slowing down the pace of things might not be so bad in the long run.

Now, for a better comparison of river barges, railroad cars and large semis, one normal river barge, which is approximately 195 ft. long and 35 ft. wide, has an approximately 1,500 ton (3 million pounds) load capacity. One railroad jumbo hopper car can carry approximately 112 tons (224,000 pounds) of cargo. One large semi/tractor trailer rig can typically haul around 26 tons (52,000 pounds) of cargo. It would take four large semis to haul the contents of just one jumbo railroad hopper car, with eight tons remaining.

A normal river barge tow consists of 15 barges. An average railroad train is approximately 100 cars. The average large semi on the road is limited to one 53 ft long trailer, and usually hauls about 26 tons of cargo. Now on that basis for comparison, it works out as follows. One river barge can haul the equivalent total weight of what can be carried in approximately 13 ½ railroad jumbo hopper cars, or the average maximum load capacity of 58 large semis. A further comparison is this, one normal tow of river barges, consisting of 15 barges can haul the equivalent weight of about two one hundred car rail trains carry, or the average maximum capacity of 870 large semis. One of the biggest advantages of using rivers and lakes and inland or inter - coastal waterways, is that rivers or none of the others mentioned ever need paving or repairs. And, by the way, no bridge repairs, another considerable advantage. Yes, some occasional dredging and repairs to locks and dams is needed, but compared to highway repairs it's 'no contest'. Overloading barges does no damage to rivers; it only makes the tow boat that pushes the barges work a little harder. As well, one modern day riverboat tow consisting of 15 normal barges, when loaded to maximum weight capacity is probably carrying around 22,500 tons of cargo. It would take approximately 870 semi trucks to haul this much on our roads.

If more products were shipped on our rivers and waterways, think of the fewer numbers of trucks on our roads. Think of less wear and tear on our bridges, think of the potential reduced air pollution. Another consideration is that unlike highway trucks, towboats and tows of barges seldom collide.

Following is another thought, what if the government was to give a tax advantage to those who ship products on the waterways? If done, this could result in increased river/waterways traffic very likely much less wear and tear on our ailing/failing roads and bridges. Yes, I know, but let me repeat, 'Common Sense'. However, Ben's precise quote was, "Common sense is all too uncommon."

Chapter 14

"Shipping by Air?"

Shipping products by air should not be overlooked. Shipping via the airways takes much strain away from roads and bridges. While it's true that trucks are needed to get airfreight to the air terminals, from there to the next ground destination there is no strain or wear and tear to our roads and bridges. As well, many people are not aware of the fact that modern day cargo planes often carry cargo weighing as much as a large eighteen-wheeled semi-truck can haul.

Most people do not realize that many products they receive or buy was transported by air.

Yes, here again, if the government was to give a tax incentive or tax advantage to those that ship by air wouldn't this very likely result in some relief to our ailing/failing roads and bridges?

It should be plain to most anyone that our over-crowded roads in their current state of repair could benefit greatly if more alternate methods of shipping were used.

Chapter 15

"An Excellent Way to Pay for Repairs"

The following is very probably the most feasible, practical and quickest way to help finance the rebuilding and maintenance of our overworked 'ailing/failing' system of roads and bridges. Quite simply, the ones that need them the most should pay their fair share. Said another way, "Those that need our roads the most, should be the ones who pay the most!"

Our Country is burdened with a huge fiscal deficit. Said in simpler terms, we do not have vast amounts of cash on hand. As well, it is very unlikely that our country could raise vast amounts of money without paying a very high rate of interest. So, instead of our government borrowing from other nations or taxing our own citizens even more, why not get some much needed help from the ones that need our road system nearly as much as we do? After all, we are always helping other countries, why not arrange a way for them to help us?

Here are some thoughts on raising revenue for our never-ending, ongoing struggle to pay for vital road and bridge repairs and re-construction. I don't mean to be unkind to our foreign neighbors and trading partners, but consider the following. It is a well-known fact that America's manufacturing industries have been going to China, Japan, Korea and various other countries worldwide far too much, and far too often. Of course this results in lost jobs and lost income for far too many Americans. Further, this results in less taxes being paid to our government, which in turn results in shortages and less money available for road and bridge maintenance and rebuilding. In view of this, I propose a perfectly fair and equitable system to be put in place so that those foreign manufacturers would have a method in which to help, or to share in our road/bridge rebuilding efforts. You know, I feel that they would be eager to help us.

You don't need to be a rocket scientist or be highly educated to understand that a majority of the products shipped to America from foreign countries arrives at our seaports. A large part of it arrives on our West coast. A very large part comes from China, Japan and Korea, a huge percentage of the large trucks on the roads coming from our West coast are hauling cargo that originates in these three countries. Simply said, we our wearing out our roads hauling freight from China, Japan, Korea and a few more. Yes, they are doing their fair share of using up our roads etc. These foreign shippers need our highway system to get their products to their final destinations, you know, 'Wally Worlds' and many others like them.

I suggest a way for these off shore businesses to participate in helping us repair and rebuild our ageing roads and bridges. Obviously our highway system is a very necessary part of their total operation to deliver their goods to their biggest and best customer, The United States of America. In view of this, I propose that we pass legislation, or heck, even an executive order, to track these foreign shipments and add on a 'road rebuilding surcharge' to these shippers, to help us help them to get their goods to the final destination. They need us, and I'm sure they'd like to participate. Why, in a way we'd be making them an offer that they couldn't refuse. What would Ben Franklin think about this?

Please let me add that in no way do I intend to suggest that the above-mentioned paragraphs are aimed at our neighboring countries that border us by land. The United States and Canada have a very good working relationship concerning trucking, roads etc. As well, we seem to have a similar situation with our neighbor to the south, Mexico, which works reasonably well, at present.

Chapter 16

"If We Can't Maintain Our Roads?"

If we can't afford to build or re-build our roads and bridges, then perhaps there are those from other countries, with more expertise, business skills and money that could do it for us? Wow! Does this sound Un-American? Does this sound like a radical idea? Well People, guess what, it has already been happening for some time, and is a growing trend. Simply said, if we aren't clever enough to make our infrastructure work, perhaps those with more expertise can.

No, this is not a Fairy Tale, it has been happening in America for some time and far too many people are not aware of it. Roads and bridges built by U.S. taxpayers are being sold off, or sometimes leased to others. So far foreign – owned companies are doing the buying or leasing.

Toll roads are certainly nothing new. History says that one of the earliest toll roads existed as far back as the seventh century B.C., or approximately 2700 years ago. Some toll roads were privately owned. While some were owned by municipalities, countries or kingdoms, in America we are richly blessed with toll roads, and will probably have many more in the future.

I personally do not feel it is right, or fair, for a state to sell a state owned road, paid for by taxpayers, to private investors to be run for profit.

I had previously heard about The State of Indiana leasing the Indiana Toll Road to an Australian-Spanish partnership, for 99 years. I didn't believe it at first, but it was true. At least they didn't sell it, in only 99 years The State of Indiana gets it back.

Now I am told that in the same day that the Indiana Toll Road deal was done, $3.8 billion for a 99-year lease, two more very important road deals were made. An Australian company bought a 99-year lease on The State of Virginia's Pocahontas Parkway. Also, on the same day, The State of Texas decided that a Spanish-American partnership could build a toll road from Austin, Texas to Seguin, Texas and run it and collect the tolls for 50 years. Yes, all these transactions occurred on just one single day. Wow, is that progress or what.

Very few people are aware the tolls collected from the U.S. side of the tunnel that connects Detroit, Michigan and Windsor; Ontario Canada goes to a subsidiary of an Australian company. As well, this same company owns a bridge in Alabama.

The city of Chicago, Illinois sold a 99-year lease on The Chicago Skyway, which is 8 miles long, for a reported $1.83 billion. The buyer was the same partnership that leased the Indiana Toll

Road. Now get braced, the company's name is quite impressive, It is, Macquarie Infrastructure Group of Sydney, Australia, and Cintra Concessiones de Infraestructuras de Transporte of Madrid, Spain.

Aside from the partnership's name being impressive, another impressing fact was that Skyway tolls rose 50 cents, to $2.50, and is predicted to be $5.00 by the year 2017. Yes, I'm sure that motorists in the Chicago area are quite impressed. One un-named Politician openly said that the tolls had needed to be raised for some time, but it would have been 'political suicide 'for a politician to suggest the toll rises. If he did, he would never get re-elected, but now, someone else is doing it so he, the politician is 'home free, or blameless'. Yes they will sell us down the tube, or do whatever they have to do, just so they can be re-elected. Pay attention Voters! They value their own re-election more than the common good of those they supposedly represent.

At present there are at least 12 or 13 states in the process of making lease or sell deals on road and bridges. Also some are exploring possibilities of selling or leasing rights to whatever company or organization that wants to build toll roads and bridges.

Alaska is said to be seeking approx. $600 million to build a proposed bridge that would connect

Anchorage, Alaska to Point Mackenzie, Alaska. It would be named the Knit Arm Bridge.

Colorado is reported to be considering a proposal from The Front Range Toll Road Company, to build a 210-mile toll road from Wellington, Colorado to close to Pueblo, Colorado.

Florida, The Tampa-Hillsborough Expressway Authority is requesting proposals from investors to build a 3.1 mile toll road connecting Interstate 275 and downtown Tampa. The estimated project cost is $150 million.

Illinois is said to be seeking ways to privatize the 274 mile long Illinois Tollway.

Indiana may want a private company to build a $1.8 billion, 142-mile extension of Interstate 69, from Indianapolis to Evansville and then manage it as a toll road.

Missouri legislature approved a plan to build a $910 million dollar bridge between St. Louis and Illinois involving a public-private partnership, with the right to collect tolls.

Nevada, a study is said to be underway on the possibility of a privately financed and privately operated 10-mile toll road the new junction of Interstates 93 and 95and the new Hoover Dam Bypass Bridge.

New Jersey Legislature is considering selling 49% of the Garden State parkway, which is 173 miles long, and The New Jersey Turnpike, which is 148 miles long, to private investors.

New York is said to be seeking Legislative changes to allow the privatization of The Long Island Expressway and The Tappan Zee Bridge. Existing laws would need to be changed to do this.

Ohio is said to be entertaining proposals from private investors to buy a 99-year lease on the Ohio Turnpike for from between $4 billion and $6 billion. The Ohio Turnpike is 241 miles long.

Oregon is said to have invited a group of investors, led by Macquarie, to assess the feasibility of 3 toll road projects and several other projects.

Texas has already done a toll road deal on a 40-mile long toll road from Austin, Texas, To Seguin, Texas for a reported $1.3 billion with private investors. Texas also made a $7.2 billion deal with the Spanish-American consortium, Cintra-Zachry to develop a 600-mile long toll road from Oklahoma to Mexico and the Gulf Coast, running parallel to existing Interstate 35.

Virginia was negotiating and may have the following deal started or done by now. It's with an American- Australian Partnership, Fluo Construction, based in California, and TranUurban Group, based in Melbourne,

Australia. The toll road deal was reportedly an approximately $913 million project.

Yes, it seems the foreign investors are having a 'field day' buying up our infrastructure. But I guess if we Americans don't have the expertise and business skills to do the projects and make them profitable someone else will do it for us. I know that many reading about these deals won't believe it, but it is true. I am reasonably sure that these foreign investors don't operate like 'The Good Fairy'. They wouldn't raise the tolls higher, would they? As well, I'm betting that they will pay their fair share of taxes to our governments. They surely will, won't they?

Chapter 17

"Some Reasons for Current Conditions"

First off, please let me say, "We have, in my opinion, the best country in the world, with the best system of operation, so far." However, even the best system so far has some flaws, after all, no system is perfect. Some prime examples follow. First and foremost is the fact that we often place people in charge of very important parts or departments of our government, sometimes even though they have no experience or much knowledge pertaining to the part they are in charge of. The first example of that comes to mind is that of 'Commander in Chief of our Armed Forces', which is of course, The President of the United States of America. By tradition, whoever is elected as President automatically becomes Commander in Chief of our Armed Forces. There is no requirement for the Commander In Chief to have any previous military experience, even one day, or for that fact, possess any provable knowledge of military activities. Yes indeed, a scary thought, in charge, but no knowledge or experience in that field. Our country has been very lucky in that regard, for the majority of our past presidents have had at least some military experience.

So, considering the previous paragraph, one would think it only logical or commonsense that a person in charge of a department or section of our government would have knowledge or be experienced in his or her field of administration? Yes, many others and I believe it should be that way, but it is not necessarily so. Most of the people in charge of important parts of our government, for instance those concerning roads and transportation, are appointed to those positions. Not all, but some, are not qualified in their fields. Far too many are appointed as a reward for their party loyalty and fund-raising efforts. Even so, they are in charge.

I am in no way suggesting that most of those in charge of our nation's roads and bridges are not qualified in their chosen fields. Most are very well qualified and dedicated. However, if some lower-level person were to point out weaknesses or needed repairs to certain sections of roads or certain bridges, he or she might well be 'squelched' in their recommendations. And very likely by someone in charge who was appointed, not for his or her expertise, but rather for their 'fund-raising abilities'.

To carry these thoughts a step further, even when those in charge are competent, on target and know what needs done, concerning roads and bridges for instance, they are constrained by those 'higher up in the food chain', meaning those that appropriate the money for the needed projects. If those higher-ups have different 'favorite' or 'pet projects' that they deem more important than fixing roads and bridges, roads and bridges might very well be put on the back burner.

It is said that there is at least one more reason for our roads and bridges being in the condition that they are. I do not know how widespread this is, or how often this happens, but I have heard that the following scenario happens. A contractor builds, or rebuilds a road or bridge, and those in charge approve the completed project and approve payment for the project. Then, it becomes apparent that the job or work was not completed as well as it should have been. Instead of calling the contractor back to correct the sub-standard work, as should be the case, I am told that far too often the maintenance people of the roads and bridges are ordered to correct the shoddy work that should have been done by the contractor. Of course, the original contractor does not pay for the corrections or repairs. Obviously this un-necessarily depletes funds that should have been available for normal maintenance. All the above could possibly be due to poor management. As well it could be the result of 'payola', or 'sweetheart deals' between those in charge and contractors. In any case, the taxpaying public, motorists and road transportation people end up with poorly maintained roads and bridges in many cases. Perhaps more oversight is needed in this regard.

It is no secret that there are many legislators and high government officials that place much more importance on foreign nation building than that of maintaining or re-building our system of roads and bridges. Our infrastructure is vital if our country is to survive. Foreign nation building should not be the top priority. If there ever comes a day when traffic quits running on America's roads, America will stop running!

Chapter 18

"Once Again, the Reasons for This Book"

As said at the beginning of this book, this is not a 're-construction plan' for our infrastructure of roads and bridges. That will have to be formulated by those much smarter than me. Also this will require massive amounts of money. Rather this book is only a collection of some simple, obvious and commonsense ideas and suggestions that could or should give a little 'extension of useful life' to America's roads and bridges. Most of these ideas or changes could be put in place at very little or even no cost to American taxpayers. As this book's title implies, "A Reprieve Plan For Our Ailing/Failing Roads and Bridges". Obviously many of them are currently under a 'death sentence' now and need all the help we can give to them.

Perhaps now would be a good time for a better or clearer definition of the word 'reprieve'. Dictionaries give several meanings to this word, some of which follow. Among these defining words are these; breather, relief, respite, as well as the words clemency, delay and stay. As well, the word definitions pertaining to the word 'stay', include delay, stop or suspend. Therefore, I think my word choice of 'reprieve' fits best, relating to roads and bridges.

Currently, many of our roads and bridges are under a death sentence, of sorts, if changes are not brought about soon. These changes could result in a delay or stay of execution, or clemency for some of these roads and bridges in that they might have a useful life for a little longer.

I think that all the previous words and statements boil down to four simple facts:

1. Many of our roads and bridges need help and attention now!
2. Our nation does not seem to have the necessary money at this time.
3. Even if we had the money, the needed projects will take much time.
4. So, in the meantime, we need to 'buy some time', give a reprieve to our ailing/failing roads and bridges by making some much needed rule changes regarding the use of our nation's roads and bridges. These changes should help them last a little longer while financing and construction gets underway. Yes, once again, 'commonsense'.

In writing this book, I want it clearly understood that my years of experience being a trucker on our nation's highways for approximately 43 years, and observing the ever-changing conditions of our

highway system is the basis for me writing this book.

I do not claim to be college educated or to be an engineering genius. Our country is richly blessed with well-qualified people to do the complicated stuff. I am quite sure that many of these competent highway engineers, planners, etc. are well aware of the changes needed to help our roads and bridges last a little longer. However, as I pointed out previously, too many of these competent people are reluctant to put forth ideas such as mine, because it might not be what their superiors want to hear, in short, they are afraid to speak out. I am under no threat of losing my position for speaking my mind, so I'm saying what I think needs to be said. I am only offering simple, obvious, practical and commonsense ideas and suggestions that could help our nation's traffic and commerce keep running while the major re-construction and financing is arranged and worked out.

Also, I'd like to say that if any single thought or suggestion in this book results in even one bridge not collapsing or even one person not being killed or injured, then I will feel that the work involved in writing this was well worthwhile.

Chapter 19

"A Summary of These Ideas and Suggestions"

These ideas and suggestions are not super complicated, actually they are super simple. The super complicated part comes later in raking up the necessary money to properly rebuild or fix these roads and bridges. Our country is richly blessed with good engineers and construction specialists, who are quite capable of doing the job right. If only the politicians and bureaucrats can see and understand the need for these projects to begin. In the meantime, we need to implement the plan to give a 'reprieve', or 'an extension of life' to our ailing, failing roads and bridges. It's not complicated; on the contrary the plan is very simple. I'm sure that there will be those that will say in one way or another, "Oh yes, those are good ideas about the roads and bridges, but let's wait awhile before using those ideas." I say, "Let's not wait and cross that bridge when we come to it, because it might not still be standing." Some might say, "Oh, it's too late now, that's water under the bridge!" However it might be the case that the bridge is under the water!

The most complicated part of this 'reprieve' plan will most likely be that of the bureaucrats trying to find a way to profit by, or 'cash in' on these proposed plans and changes. If done right, there should be no way for anyone to profit from this plan, other than profiting from our roads and bridges possibly lasting a bit longer. That certainly could be a very valuable benefit.

Let us not forget that America's vast network of roads and bridges are a National Treasure, and as a whole, the best in the world. As well, our transportation system is vital to our country. If we can make any part of this vast network last a little longer by implementing simple commonsense (there I said it again), rules and changes, how could we possibly lose? These fore mentioned ideas and suggestions could all be implemented, carried out, and administered by existing governmental agencies, with no need for additional personnel or offices or buildings. Commonsense should tell most anyone that all the people and facilities needed to put this 'Bridges/Roads/Reprieve' plan in effect already exist.

Chapter 20

"Some Recent Infrastructure Plans"

On Jan. 12, 2015, the government announced new infrastructure planning that was in the works. Transportation Secretary Anthony Foxx unveiled a huge 30 year plan, still being formulated, which would deal with our existing infrastructure problems as well as our transportation system in general. It is a far reaching plan to accommodate future growth of population in certain areas, as well as shifts in current heavily populated areas.

Remember, this is 30 year plan, and it will take many billions of dollars to accomplish the plan's goals. The ASCE (American Society of Civil Engineers) said two years ago that it would take an approximately $3.6 trillion investment by 2020 to meet infrastructure needs. As well, they figure that at the current rate of spending, the money will fall about $1.6 trillion short.

The Miller Center at the University of Virginia, and the American Society of Civil Engineers said that just maintaining infrastructure at current levels would require additional spending of $134 billion to $194 billion each year through the year of 2035. Yes, they said each year!

At present our leaders are working on ways to replenish the depleted Federal Highway Trust Fund. Of course, this is critical and very necessary.

O.K., well and good, they are working on a plan, and as said it is a 30 year plan.

In the meantime, why not implement some of my suggestions in this book? Perhaps these very simple, low cost and no cost ideas could result in buying a little time, or adding some useful life for our Ailing/Failing Roads and Bridges.

"A Quick Review of This Book's Contents"

By chapter:

1. Condition of our roads and bridges

2. History of the Interstate Highway System

3,4, & 5: Why roads and bridges are failing

6. Some possible remedies by re-routing etc.

7. An overview of our road's conditions

8. Some possible emergency back-up plans

9. Some lane change suggestions

10. Truck overloads not main problem

11. One reason for so many trucks

12,13, & 14: Consider other transport modes

15. A way to finance re-construction

16. Other ways to manage our roads etc.

As I said at the beginning of this little book, my plan and suggestions will very likely be ignored by those in charge, probably because of the lack of the potential to 'cash in' on them. However, I am making sure that the right people receive a copy of this book. At least then, I'll know that they know.

All publicity concerning this book would be very helpful and very much appreciated. As well, any and all feedback from reviewers and critics would also be appreciated.

Thanks for taking the time to read it.

Other books, e-books and audio books

From: JIM HUBLER
aka
William James Hubler Jr.

At Amazon.com and

Barnes & Noble

The Cliffs of Leavenworth ISBN 978-1-4120-7490-2

Some Trucking Tales (Volume 1) ISBN 9 787774 558272

The Kentucky Corn Cob Wine Connoisseur ISBN 978-0-9847201-2-5

Political Poetry at the Poor Poet's Pub Primarily Picking on Professional Politicians and Other Hard-Core Unemployables ISBN 978-0-9847201-0-1

Some Poems and Such with a Farming Touch ISBN 978-0-9847201-9-4

ALSO: JIM HUBLER's MUSIC

AVAILABLE ON CDs, DVDs, and mp3 format

From Amazon.com and CD BABY Online Music Store.
Also available at most mp3 Sites Online, YouTube, Facebook, Twitter & JIMHUBLERWEB.com

About the Author

Jim Hubler is an ex-Hoosier now living in Kentucky. He lives near the village of Wolf Creek, in Meade County Kentucky, in the back-woods on a high bluff overlooking the beautiful Ohio River. He retired from being a truck driver, but not from being a writer. He still writes books, poetry, songs and articles. As well, he is an avid guitar enthusiast (guitar owner), plays guitar part-time with a couple of groups, and records some of his self- penned songs, with the help of some of his very talented friends.

Jim's interests are many and varied. He likes dogs, big trucks, good guitars (Gibsons mostly), and many kinds of music. He writes about everything he likes, plus more. He loves the humorous side of life, but also writes some things 'as serious as a heart attack'. His main rule of life is, "Never Trust a Man That Don't like Dogs."

Jim is a member, or affiliated with the following organizations or groups:

Retired Teamster, Local #135,
Indianapolis, Indiana
Member of Teamster Local #135 Retirees Club
American Truck Historical Society
Broadcast Music Inc. (BMI) Songwriter
Kentucky State Poetry Society
Breckinridge Bluegrass Music Association
Natl. Thumbpickers Hall of Fame Assoc.
PINs Society (Pets in Need Society)
Harrison Masonic Lodge #122
Valley of Louisville, Ky. Scottish Rite
Kosair Shrine, Louisville, Ky.
32nd Division Veteran Assoc. (Wisconsin)
32nd Division Oldtimers Club
Red Arrow Club of Southern Wis.
NRA (National Rifle Association)

www.ingramcontent.com/pod-product-compliance
Lightning Source LLC
Chambersburg PA
CBHW032050040426
42449CB00007B/1058